German - Norwegian

Teach Your Child to Read

700 Short Easy Sentences

Name

I Can...

- [ ] read the 1st sentence.
- [ ] read the 2nd sentence.
- [ ] read the 3rd sentence.
- [ ] make my own sentence.
- [ ] color a picture.

Der Frosch geht auf eine Party.

Frosken skal på fest.

The frog is going to a party.

Der grüne Frosch trägt einen grünen Hut.

Den grønne frosken har på seg en grønn hatt.

The green frog is wearing a green hat.

Name

I Can...

- [ ] read the 1st sentence.
- [ ] read the 2nd sentence.
- [ ] read the 3rd sentence.
- [ ] make my own sentence.
- [ ] color a picture.

Eule liest gern große Bücher.

Uglen liker å lese store bøker.

Owl likes to read big books.

Die junge braune Eule lernt lesen.

Den unge brune uglen lærer å lese.

The young brown owl is learning to read.

Name

I Can...

- ☐ read the 1st sentence.
- ☐ read the 2nd sentence.
- ☐ read the 3rd sentence.
- ☐ make my own sentence.
- ☐ color a picture.

Komm schon! Der Eiswagen ist da!

Kom igjen! Isbilen er her!

Come on! The ice cream truck is here!

Der Eiswagen spielt ein schönes Lied.

Isbilen spiller en vakker sang.

The ice cream truck is playing a beautiful song.

Name

I Can...

- [ ] read the 1st sentence.
- [ ] read the 2nd sentence.
- [ ] read the 3rd sentence.
- [ ] make my own sentence.
- [ ] color a picture.

Drachen sind sehr freundlich und haben Schuppen auf dem Rücken.

Drager er veldig vennlige og har vekter på ryggen.

Dragons are very friendly and have scales on their backs.

Der große antike Drache sagt Hallo zu dir.

Den store gamle dragen sier hei til deg.

The big ancient dragon says hello to you.

Name 

I Can...

- [ ] read the 1st sentence.
- [ ] read the 2nd sentence.
- [ ] read the 3rd sentence.
- [ ] make my own sentence.
- [ ] color a picture.

Dieser Widder wohnt im Bauernhaus.

Denne rammen bor i våningshuset.

This ram lives in the farmhouse.

Der Widder lächelt, weil er gerade gebadet hat.

Rammen smiler fordi den bare tok et bad.

The ram is smiling because it just took a bath.

Name 

I Can...

- [ ] read the 1st sentence.
- [ ] read the 2nd sentence.
- [ ] read the 3rd sentence.
- [ ] make my own sentence.
- [ ] color a picture.

Der Hase isst gerne Karotten.

Bunny liker å spise gulrøtter.

The bunny likes to eat carrots.

Der Hase bringt seiner Familie eine Riesenmöhre zum Abendessen.

Bunnyen tar med seg en gigantisk gulrot til familien til middag.

The bunny is bringing a giant carrot to its family for dinner.

Name ________________________

I Can...

- [ ] read the 1st sentence.
- [ ] read the 2nd sentence.
- [ ] read the 3rd sentence.
- [ ] make my own sentence.
- [ ] color a picture.

Der Clown verschenkt gern Luftballons an kleine Kinder.

Klovnen liker å gi ut ballonger til små barn.

The clown likes to give out balloons to little kids.

Der Clown hält drei bunte Luftballons.

Klovnen holder tre fargerike ballonger.

The clown is holding three colorful balloons.

Name 

I Can...

- [ ] read the 1st sentence.
- [ ] read the 2nd sentence.
- [ ] read the 3rd sentence.
- [ ] make my own sentence.
- [ ] color a picture.

Der Clown jongliert Bälle für seine Leistung.

Klovnen sjonglerer baller for sin prestasjon.

The clown is juggling balls for his performance.

Der lustige Clown jongliert mit Geschicklichkeit.

Den morsomme klovnen sjonglerer med dyktighet.

The funny clown is juggling with skill.

Name ___________________ 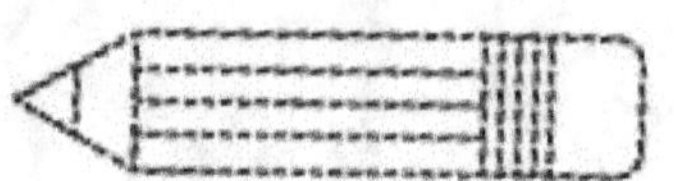

I Can...

- [ ] read the 1st sentence.
- [ ] read the 2nd sentence.
- [ ] read the 3rd sentence.
- [ ] make my own sentence.
- [ ] color a picture.

Der Osterhase wird Schokoladeneier ausgeben.

Påskeharen kommer til å gi ut sjokoladeegg.

The Easter Bunny is going to give out chocolate eggs.

Das Kaninchen pflückte gerade ein paar Karotten aus dem Garten.

Kaninen plukket bare noen gulrøtter ut av hagen.

The rabbit just plucked some carrots out of the garden.

Name

I Can...

- [ ] read the 1st sentence.
- [ ] read the 2nd sentence.
- [ ] read the 3rd sentence.
- [ ] make my own sentence.
- [ ] color a picture.

Der Bleistift zeichnet eine Zick-Zack-Linie.

Blyanten tegner en sikksakk-linje.

The pencil is drawing a zig-zag line.

Der Bleistift kritzelt eine Linie mit der Mine.

Blyanten skritter en linje med ledningen.

The pencil is scribbling a line with the lead.

Name 

I Can...

- [ ] read the 1st sentence.
- [ ] read the 2nd sentence.
- [ ] read the 3rd sentence.
- [ ] make my own sentence.
- [ ] color a picture.

Der Bleistift setzte ein breites Lächeln auf und machte sich an die Arbeit.

Blyanten la på seg et stort smil og gikk på jobb.

The pencil put on a big smile and went to work.

Der Stift wacht hell und früh auf, um zur Arbeit zu gehen.

Blyanten våkner lyst og tidlig for å gå på jobb.

The pencil wakes up bright and early to go to work.

Name

I Can...

- [ ] read the 1st sentence.
- [ ] read the 2nd sentence.
- [ ] read the 3rd sentence.
- [ ] make my own sentence.
- [ ] color a picture.

Dieser Schneemann ist mein Freund und er ist ein Helfer des Weihnachtsmanns.

Denne snømannen er min venn, og han er en hjelper til julenissen.

This snowman is my friend, and he is a helper of Santa.

Der Schneemann feiert Weihnachten.

Snømannen holder julebord.

The snowman is having a Christmas party.

Name ____________________ 

I Can...

- [ ] read the 1st sentence.
- [ ] read the 2nd sentence.
- [ ] read the 3rd sentence.
- [ ] make my own sentence.
- [ ] color a picture.

Die Krake arbeitet als Koch und serviert Essen.

Blekkspruten jobber som kokk og serverer mat.

The octopus is working as a chef and serving food.

Der Tintenfisch kochte köstliches Essen für seine Freunde.

Blekkspruten tilberedte deilig mat til vennene sine.

The octopus cooked delicious food for its friends.

Name

I Can...

- [ ] read the 1st sentence.
- [ ] read the 2nd sentence.
- [ ] read the 3rd sentence.
- [ ] make my own sentence.
- [ ] color a picture.

Der Weihnachtsmann ist glücklich.

Julenissen er fornøyd.

Santa is happy.

Der Weihnachtsmann liefert den Kindern Geschenke.

Julenissen leverer gaver til barna.

Santa Claus is delivering presents to the children.

Name ______________________ 

I Can...

- [ ] read the 1st sentence.
- [ ] read the 2nd sentence.
- [ ] read the 3rd sentence.
- [ ] make my own sentence.
- [ ] color a picture.

Der Bär isst gerne Süßigkeiten.

Bjørnen spiser søtsaker.

The bear likes to eat sweets.

Der braune Teddybär trägt einen hellgrünen Hut.

Den brune bamsen har en lysegrønn hatt på.

The brown teddy bear is wearing a bright green hat.

Name

I Can...

- [ ] read the 1st sentence.
- [ ] read the 2nd sentence.
- [ ] read the 3rd sentence.
- [ ] make my own sentence.
- [ ] color a picture.

Das Buch hat einen Zauberstab.

Boken har et tryllestav.

The book has a wand.

Der Junge bekam zu seinem Geburtstag eine Zauberer-Actionfigur.

Gutten fikk en trollmannshandling for bursdagen sin.

The boy got a wizard action figure for his birthday.

Name _______________________

I Can...

- [ ] read the 1st sentence.
- [ ] read the 2nd sentence.
- [ ] read the 3rd sentence.
- [ ] make my own sentence.
- [ ] color a picture.

Der Bär hat ein Geschenk.

Bjørnen har en gave.

The bear has a present.

Der Teddybär öffnet sein zweites Geschenk.

Bamsen åpner sin andre gave.

The teddy bear is opening his second present.

Name

I Can...

- [ ] read the 1st sentence.
- [ ] read the 2nd sentence.
- [ ] read the 3rd sentence.
- [ ] make my own sentence.
- [ ] color a picture.

Der Weihnachtsmann wird Geschenke verteilen.

Julenissen kommer til å gi gaver.

Santa is going to give out presents.

Der Weihnachtsmann trägt eine Ledertasche mit Geschenken.

Julenissen har med seg en skinnveske fylt med gaver.

Santa Claus is carrying a leather bag filled with gifts.

Name

I Can...

- [ ] read the 1st sentence.
- [ ] read the 2nd sentence.
- [ ] read the 3rd sentence.
- [ ] make my own sentence.
- [ ] color a picture.

Ich habe einen Schneemann gemacht.

Jeg laget en snømann.

I made a snowman.

Der Schneemann war gerade mit der Reinigung des Hofes fertig.

Snømannen var akkurat ferdig med å rense hagen.

The snowman was just done cleaning the yard.

20

I Can...

- [ ] read the 1st sentence.
- [ ] read the 2nd sentence.
- [ ] read the 3rd sentence.
- [ ] make my own sentence.
- [ ] color a picture.

Der Papagei ist bunt.

Papegøyen er fargerik.

The parrot is colorful.

Der Papagei lernt gerade, wie man am Himmel fliegt.

Papegøyen lærer bare å fly på himmelen.

The parrot is just learning how to fly in the sky.

Name ___________

I Can...

- ☐ read the 1st sentence.
- ☐ read the 2nd sentence.
- ☐ read the 3rd sentence.
- ☐ make my own sentence.
- ☐ color a picture.

Es gibt viele Tiere.

Det er mange dyr.

There are a lot of animals.

Die Tiere haben einen riesigen Schlaf.

Dyrene får en enorm søvn.

The animals are having a giant sleepover.

Name

I Can...

- [ ] read the 1st sentence.
- [ ] read the 2nd sentence.
- [ ] read the 3rd sentence.
- [ ] make my own sentence.
- [ ] color a picture.

Der Mann trägt einen Gürtel.

Mannen har belte på seg.

The man is wearing a belt.

Der Mann kommt, um das Schiff zu reparieren.

Mannen kommer for å fikse skipet.

The man is coming to fix the ship.

Name

I Can...

- [ ] read the 1st sentence.
- [ ] read the 2nd sentence.
- [ ] read the 3rd sentence.
- [ ] make my own sentence.
- [ ] color a picture.

Das Kaninchen ist sehr jung.

Kaninen er veldig ung.

The rabbit is very young.

Der Magier holte ein Kaninchen aus seinem Hut.

Trollmannen tilkalte en kanin ut av hatten.

The magician summoned a rabbit out of his hat.

Name

I Can...

- [ ] read the 1st sentence.
- [ ] read the 2nd sentence.
- [ ] read the 3rd sentence.
- [ ] make my own sentence.
- [ ] color a picture.

Er hat einen Trank.

Han har en potion.

He has a potion.

Die Frau lernt, Wissenschaftlerin zu werden.

Kvinnen lærer å bli forsker.

The woman is learning how to become a scientist.

Name

I Can...

- [ ] read the 1st sentence.
- [ ] read the 2nd sentence.
- [ ] read the 3rd sentence.
- [ ] make my own sentence.
- [ ] color a picture.

Er trägt eine Sonnenbrille.

Han har på seg solbriller.

He is wearing sunglasses.

Der Polizist ist wütend auf einige faule Teenager.

Politimannen er sint på noen råtne tenåringer.

The policeman is angry at some rotten teenagers.

Name 

I Can...

- [ ] read the 1st sentence.
- [ ] read the 2nd sentence.
- [ ] read the 3rd sentence.
- [ ] make my own sentence.
- [ ] color a picture.

Er hat einen Farbeimer.

Han har en bøtte med maling.

He has a bucket of paint.

Der Anstreicher ist fast fertig mit seiner täglichen Arbeit.

Husmaleren er nesten ferdig med sitt daglige arbeid.

The house painter is almost done with his daily work.

Name ___________________ 

I Can...

- [ ] read the 1st sentence.
- [ ] read the 2nd sentence.
- [ ] read the 3rd sentence.
- [ ] make my own sentence.
- [ ] color a picture.

Der Mann hat einen Hut.

Mannen har hatt.

The man has a hat.

Der Postbote liefert im Morgengrauen Post.

Postmannen leverer post i daggryssprikken.

The postman is delivering mails at the crack of dawn.

Name

I Can...

- [ ] read the 1st sentence.
- [ ] read the 2nd sentence.
- [ ] read the 3rd sentence.
- [ ] make my own sentence.
- [ ] color a picture.

Er hat ein Walkie-Talkie.

Han har en walkie talkie.

He has a walkie talkie.

Der Geschäftsmann ruft seinen Chef an.

Forretningsmannen ringer sjefen sin.

The businessman is calling his boss.

Name

I Can...

- [ ] read the 1st sentence.
- [ ] read the 2nd sentence.
- [ ] read the 3rd sentence.
- [ ] make my own sentence.
- [ ] color a picture.

Er ist schläfrig.

Han er søvnig.

He is sleepy.

Der Arbeiter schleppt einige schwere Kisten.

Arbeidsmannen sleper noen tunge kasser.

The workman is towing some heavy boxes.

Name _______________________ 

I Can...

- [ ] read the 1st sentence.
- [ ] read the 2nd sentence.
- [ ] read the 3rd sentence.
- [ ] make my own sentence.
- [ ] color a picture.

Er trägt eine Fliege.

Han har på seg bowie.

He is wearing a bowtie.

Der Kellner serviert einer Familie frische Limonade.

The waiter serverer fersk limonade til en familie.

The waiter is serving fresh lemonade to a family.

Name _______________

I Can...

- ☐ read the 1st sentence.
- ☐ read the 2nd sentence.
- ☐ read the 3rd sentence.
- ☐ make my own sentence.
- ☐ color a picture.

Er hat einen Koffer.

Han har koffert.

He has a suitcase.

Der Ingenieur wird ein schickes blaues Auto reparieren.

Ingeniøren skal fikse en fancy blå bil.

The engineer is going to fix a fancy blue car.

Name 

I Can...

- [ ] read the 1st sentence.
- [ ] read the 2nd sentence.
- [ ] read the 3rd sentence.
- [ ] make my own sentence.
- [ ] color a picture.

Der Koch hat eine Serviette.

Kokken har et serviett.

The chef has a napkin.

Der Küchenchef machte leckere Pasta für alle zum Teilen.

Kokken lagde kjempegod pasta for alle å dele.

The chef made yummy pasta for everyone to share.

Name

I Can...

- ☐ read the 1st sentence.
- ☐ read the 2nd sentence.
- ☐ read the 3rd sentence.
- ☐ make my own sentence.
- ☐ color a picture.

Der Hahn hat einen großen Schnabel.

Hanen har et stort nebb.

The rooster has a big beak.

Das weiße Huhn trägt einen Künstlerhut.

Den hvite kyllingen har på seg en kunstnerhatt.

The white chicken is wearing an artist's hat.

Name

I Can...

- [ ] read the 1st sentence.
- [ ] read the 2nd sentence.
- [ ] read the 3rd sentence.
- [ ] make my own sentence.
- [ ] color a picture.

Der Vogel ist klein.

Fuglen er liten.

The bird is small.

Das kleine Küken spielt mit dem Telefon seiner Mutter Musik.

Den lille kyllingen bruker sin mors telefon for å spille musikk.

The little chick is using his mother's phone to play music.

Name ____________________ 

I Can...

- [ ] read the 1st sentence.
- [ ] read the 2nd sentence.
- [ ] read the 3rd sentence.
- [ ] make my own sentence.
- [ ] color a picture.

Das ist mein Ring.

Det er ringen min.

That is my ring.

Auf dem Ring befindet sich ein Diamantjuwel.

Ringen har en diamantjuvel på seg.

The ring has a diamond jewel on it.

Name ___________

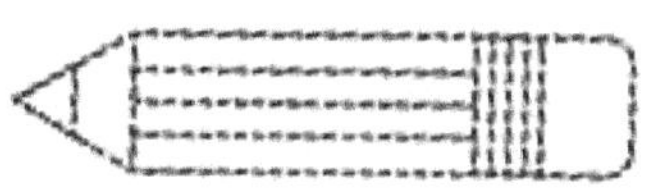

I Can...

- [ ] read the 1st sentence.
- [ ] read the 2nd sentence.
- [ ] read the 3rd sentence.
- [ ] make my own sentence.
- [ ] color a picture.

Die Ente hat drei Eier.

Anda har tre egg.

The duck has three eggs.

Die Ente ließ gerade ihre kleinen ovalen Eier fallen.

Anda droppet bare de små ovale eggene sine.

The duck just dropped its little oval eggs.

Name

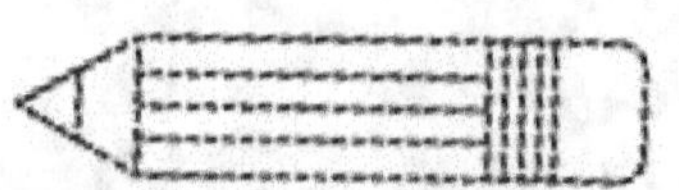

I Can...

- [ ] read the 1st sentence.
- [ ] read the 2nd sentence.
- [ ] read the 3rd sentence.
- [ ] make my own sentence.
- [ ] color a picture.

Der Schwan ist wunderschön.

Svanen er vakker.

The swan is beautiful.

Der schöne Schwan isst ein Stück grünes Gemüse.

Den vakre svanen spiser et stykke grønne grønnsaker.

The beautiful swan is eating a piece of green vegetables.

Name ___________

I Can...

- [ ] read the 1st sentence.
- [ ] read the 2nd sentence.
- [ ] read the 3rd sentence.
- [ ] make my own sentence.
- [ ] color a picture.

Das Mädchen trägt ein Kleid.

Jenta har på seg en kjole.

The girl is wearing a dress.

Das kleine Mädchen trägt zwei Eimer voll Wasser.

Den lille jenta har to vann med bøtter.

The little girl is carrying two buckets loads of water.

Name

I Can...

- [ ] read the 1st sentence.
- [ ] read the 2nd sentence.
- [ ] read the 3rd sentence.
- [ ] make my own sentence.
- [ ] color a picture.

Der Junge rennt.

Gutten løper.

The boy is running.

Der Sprinter gewinnt den ersten Platz in einem Rennen.

Sprinteren vinner førsteplassen i et løp.

The sprinter is winning first place in a race.

Name

I Can...

- [ ] read the 1st sentence.
- [ ] read the 2nd sentence.
- [ ] read the 3rd sentence.
- [ ] make my own sentence.
- [ ] color a picture.

Er ist ein Musiker.

Han er musiker.

He is a musician.

Der Junge übt die Flöte, um in der Schule fertig zu sein.

Gutten øver på fløyten for å være klar på skolen.

The boy is practicing the flute to be ready at school.

Name ________________

I Can...

- [ ] read the 1st sentence.
- [ ] read the 2nd sentence.
- [ ] read the 3rd sentence.
- [ ] make my own sentence.
- [ ] color a picture.

Er sieht fröhlich aus.

Han ser glad ut.

He looks joyful.

Der Schlagzeuger leitet eine riesige Kostümparade.

Trommeslageren leder en enorm draktparade.

The drummer is leading a huge costume parade.

Name

I Can...

- [ ] read the 1st sentence.
- [ ] read the 2nd sentence.
- [ ] read the 3rd sentence.
- [ ] make my own sentence.
- [ ] color a picture.

Der Dinosaurier ist ein Rockstar.

Dinosauren er en rockestjerne.

The dinosaur is a rock star.

Der Traum des Dinosauriers ist es, ein wundervoller Rockstar zu werden.

Dinosaurens drøm er å bli en fantastisk rockestjerne.

The dinosaur's dream is to become a wonderful rock star.

Name ____________________ 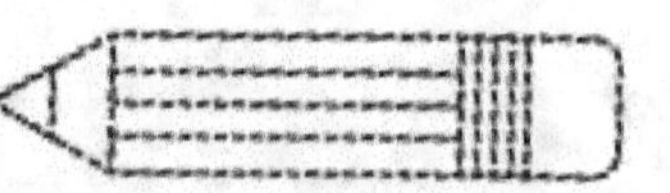

I Can...

- [ ] read the 1st sentence.
- [ ] read the 2nd sentence.
- [ ] read the 3rd sentence.
- [ ] make my own sentence.
- [ ] color a picture.

Die Krankenschwester hilft dem Arzt.

Sykepleieren hjelper legen.

The nurse helps the doctor.

Die Krankenschwester hilft den Patienten, besser zu werden.

Sykepleieren hjelper pasienter med å bli bedre.

The nurse is helping patients get better.

Name

I Can...

- [ ] read the 1st sentence.
- [ ] read the 2nd sentence.
- [ ] read the 3rd sentence.
- [ ] make my own sentence.
- [ ] color a picture.

Sie trägt eine Krone.

Hun har på seg en krone.

She is wearing a crown.

Der Bienenstock hat einen Anführer, der eine magische Biene ist.

Bikupen har en leder som er en magisk bie.

The beehive has a leader who is a magical bee.

Name

I Can...

- [ ] read the 1st sentence.
- [ ] read the 2nd sentence.
- [ ] read the 3rd sentence.
- [ ] make my own sentence.
- [ ] color a picture.

Es ist orange und schwarz.

Den er oransje og svart.

It is orange and black.

Ein formeller Tiger winkt mit der Hand nach einem gelben Taxi.

En formell tiger vifter med hånden etter en gul taxi.

A formal tiger is waving his hand for a yellow taxi.

Name

I Can...

- [ ] read the 1st sentence.
- [ ] read the 2nd sentence.
- [ ] read the 3rd sentence.
- [ ] make my own sentence.
- [ ] color a picture.

Der Junge trägt viele Bücher.

Gutten har mange bøker på seg.

The boy is carrying a lot of books.

Der kluge kleine Junge trägt schwere Bücher zum Lernen.

Den smarte lille gutten bærer tunge bøker for å studere.

The smart little boy is carrying heavy books to study.

Name

I Can...

- [ ] read the 1st sentence.
- [ ] read the 2nd sentence.
- [ ] read the 3rd sentence.
- [ ] make my own sentence.
- [ ] color a picture.

Die Pizza sieht köstlich aus.

Pizzaen ser deilig ut.

The pizza looks delicious.

Der Koch nahm gerade den Pizzaofen

Kokken tok nettopp pizzaovnen

The chef just took the pizza oven

Name

I Can...

- [ ] read the 1st sentence.
- [ ] read the 2nd sentence.
- [ ] read the 3rd sentence.
- [ ] make my own sentence.
- [ ] color a picture.

Das ist der Computer meines Vaters.

Det er datamaskinen til faren min.

That is my dad's computer.

Der Laptop begrüßt den Benutzer.

Den bærbare datamaskinen sier hei til brukeren.

The laptop is saying hi to the user.

Name

I Can...

- [ ] read the 1st sentence.
- [ ] read the 2nd sentence.
- [ ] read the 3rd sentence.
- [ ] make my own sentence.
- [ ] color a picture.

Der Bauer hat einen Bart.

Bonden har skjegg.

The farmer has a beard.

Der Gärtner wird einige Samen pflanzen.

Gartneren skal plante noen frø.

The gardener is going to plant some seeds.

Name ___________

I Can...

- [ ] read the 1st sentence.
- [ ] read the 2nd sentence.
- [ ] read the 3rd sentence.
- [ ] make my own sentence.
- [ ] color a picture.

Die Erdbeere ist rot.

Jordbæren er rød.

The strawberry is red.

Die Erdbeere trinkt kalten erfrischenden Saft.

Jordbæren drikker kald forfriskende juice.

The strawberry is drinking cold refreshing juice.

Name

I Can...

- [ ] read the 1st sentence.
- [ ] read the 2nd sentence.
- [ ] read the 3rd sentence.
- [ ] make my own sentence.
- [ ] color a picture.

Der Zauberer hat einen Zauberstab.

Trollmannen har en tryllestav.

The magician has a wand.

Der Zauberer wird einen großen Drachen beschwören.

Veiviseren skal tilkalle en flott stor drage.

The wizard is going to summon a great big dragon.

Name _______________________

I Can...

- [ ] read the 1st sentence.
- [ ] read the 2nd sentence.
- [ ] read the 3rd sentence.
- [ ] make my own sentence.
- [ ] color a picture.

Rentier hat einen Schal.

Reinsdyr har et skjerf.

Reindeer has a scarf.

Das Rentier kommt zu spät, um seinen Freunden sein Geschenk zu geben.

Reinen er sent ute med å gi sin gave til vennene sine.

The reindeer is late to give his present to his friends.

Name _______________________

I Can...

- [ ] read the 1st sentence.
- [ ] read the 2nd sentence.
- [ ] read the 3rd sentence.
- [ ] make my own sentence.
- [ ] color a picture.

Ich habe viele Stifte.

Jeg har mange blyanter.

I have a lot of pencils.

Die Schreibgeräte befinden sich in der Blechdose.

Skriveutstyrene er i blikkboksen.

The writing utensils are in the tin can.

Name 

I Can...

- [ ] read the 1st sentence.
- [ ] read the 2nd sentence.
- [ ] read the 3rd sentence.
- [ ] make my own sentence.
- [ ] color a picture.

Der Weihnachtsmann ist fett.

Julenissen er feit.

Santa is fat.

Der Weihnachtsmann lacht über einen lustigen Witz.

Julenissen ler av en morsom vits.

Santa Claus is laughing at a hilarious joke.

Name ____________________

I Can...

- [ ] read the 1st sentence.
- [ ] read the 2nd sentence.
- [ ] read the 3rd sentence.
- [ ] make my own sentence.
- [ ] color a picture.

Ich habe eine Nase.

Jeg har en nese.

I have one nose.

Nummer eins belegte bei einem Wettbewerb den ersten Platz.

Nummer én fikk førsteplass på en konkurranse.

Number one got first place at a competition.

Name

I Can...

- [ ] read the 1st sentence.
- [ ] read the 2nd sentence.
- [ ] read the 3rd sentence.
- [ ] make my own sentence.
- [ ] color a picture.

Ich habe zwei Ohren.

Jeg har to ører.

I have two ears.

Nummer zwei posiert für ein Selfie.

Nummer to poserer for en selfie.

Number two is posing for a selfie.

I Can...

- [ ] read the 1st sentence.
- [ ] read the 2nd sentence.
- [ ] read the 3rd sentence.
- [ ] make my own sentence.
- [ ] color a picture.

Ich habe drei Knöpfe an meinem Kleid.

Jeg har tre knapper på kjolen.

I have three buttons on my dress.

Nummer drei zählt bis drei.

Nummer tre teller til tre.

Number three is counting to three.

Name ___________

I Can...

- [ ] read the 1st sentence.
- [ ] read the 2nd sentence.
- [ ] read the 3rd sentence.
- [ ] make my own sentence.
- [ ] color a picture.

Ich habe 0 Schwänze.

Jeg har 0 haler.

I have 0 tails.

Die Null sagt gut, indem sie die OK-Geste macht.

Nullen sier fint ved å gjøre den ok gesten.

The zero is saying fine by making the okay gesture.

Name ___________________ 

I Can...

- [ ] read the 1st sentence.
- [ ] read the 2nd sentence.
- [ ] read the 3rd sentence.
- [ ] make my own sentence.
- [ ] color a picture.

Ich habe fünf Finger an einer meiner Hände.

Jeg har fem fingre på 1 av hendene.

I have five fingers on 1 of my hands.

Die fünf sagen laut ihren Namen, damit andere es wissen.

De fem sier navnet sitt høyt, så andre vil vite det.

The five are saying its name out loud, so others will know.

Name _______________________

I Can...

- ☐ read the 1st sentence.
- ☐ read the 2nd sentence.
- ☐ read the 3rd sentence.
- ☐ make my own sentence.
- ☐ color a picture.

Meine Katze hat vier Beine.

Katten min har fire bein.

My cat has four legs.

Die vier sahen vier Delfine am Meer.

De fire så fire delfiner ved havet.

The four saw four dolphins at the ocean.

Name

I Can...

- [ ] read the 1st sentence.
- [ ] read the 2nd sentence.
- [ ] read the 3rd sentence.
- [ ] make my own sentence.
- [ ] color a picture.

Ein Schmetterling hat sechs Beine.

En sommerfugl har seks ben.

A butterfly has six legs.

Die sechs springen aufgeregt auf und ab.

De seks hopper spent opp og ned.

The six are excitedly jumping up and down.

Name _______________

I Can...

- [ ] read the 1st sentence.
- [ ] read the 2nd sentence.
- [ ] read the 3rd sentence.
- [ ] make my own sentence.
- [ ] color a picture.

Eine Spinne hat acht Beine.

En edderkopp har åtte ben.

A spider has eight legs.

Die Acht leckt sich über die Lippen, weil sie acht Iabletts mit gebratenem Hühnchen sieht.

De åtte slikker leppen fordi den ser åtte brett med stekt kylling.

The eight is licking its lip because it sees eight trays of fried chicken.

Name ____________________ 

I Can...

- [ ] read the 1st sentence.
- [ ] read the 2nd sentence.
- [ ] read the 3rd sentence.
- [ ] make my own sentence.
- [ ] color a picture.

Der Hahn wird die Leute wecken.

Hanen skal vekke folk.

The rooster is going to wake people up.

Der Hahn weckt alle auf.

Hanen våkner opp alle sammen.

The rooster is waking up everybody.

Name

I Can...

- [ ] read the 1st sentence.
- [ ] read the 2nd sentence.
- [ ] read the 3rd sentence.
- [ ] make my own sentence.
- [ ] color a picture.

Meine Schwester hat neun Kuscheltiere.

Søsteren min har ni utstoppede dyr.

My sister has nine stuffed animals.

Die Neun sagt, dass $4 + 5 = 9$.

De ni sier at $4 + 5 = 9$.

The nine is saying that $4+5=9$.

Name

I Can...

- [ ] read the 1st sentence.
- [ ] read the 2nd sentence.
- [ ] read the 3rd sentence.
- [ ] make my own sentence.
- [ ] color a picture.

Das Bienenbaby hat gelbe und schwarze Streifen.

Babybien har gule og svarte striper.

The baby bee has yellow and black stripes.

Die Babybienen haben sehr kleine Flügel.

Babybiene har veldig små vinger.

The baby bees have very tiny wings.

Name

I Can...

- [ ] read the 1st sentence.
- [ ] read the 2nd sentence.
- [ ] read the 3rd sentence.
- [ ] make my own sentence.
- [ ] color a picture.

Der Marienkäfer hat viele Stellen.

Marihøna har mange flekker.

The ladybug has many spots.

Der Marienkäfer isst ein Stück Salat.

Marihøna spiser et stykke salat.

The ladybug is eating a piece of lettuce.

Name

I Can...

- [ ] read the 1st sentence.
- [ ] read the 2nd sentence.
- [ ] read the 3rd sentence.
- [ ] make my own sentence.
- [ ] color a picture.

Die Schafe sind dünn.

Sauene er tynne.

The sheep are skinny.

Dieses Schaf ist so flauschig.

Denne sauen er så luftig.

This sheep is so fluffy.

Name

I Can...

- [ ] read the 1st sentence.
- [ ] read the 2nd sentence.
- [ ] read the 3rd sentence.
- [ ] make my own sentence.
- [ ] color a picture.

Der Hase nimmt an einem Eiermalwettbewerb teil.

Kaninen deltar i en eggmalingskonkurranse.

The rabbit is entering an egg painting contest.

Der Osterhase malt gerne Eier.

Påskeharen liker å male egg.

The Easter Bunny likes to paint eggs.

Name

I Can...

- [ ] read the 1st sentence.
- [ ] read the 2nd sentence.
- [ ] read the 3rd sentence.
- [ ] make my own sentence.
- [ ] color a picture.

Die Eule ist Sprachlehrerin.

Uglen er en lærer i språkkunster.

The owl is a language arts teacher.

Mr.Owl unterrichtet die 3. Klasse.

Mr.Owl underviser i 3. klasse.

Mr.Owl teaches the 3rd grade.

Name

I Can...

- [ ] read the 1st sentence.
- [ ] read the 2nd sentence.
- [ ] read the 3rd sentence.
- [ ] make my own sentence.
- [ ] color a picture.

Der Mann hat einen alten Hammer.

Mannen har en eldgammel hammer.

The man has an ancient hammer.

Der Mann hat einen glänzenden neuen Hammer gekauft.

Mannen har kjøpt en skinnende ny hammer.

The man has bought a shiny new hammer.

Name ____________________ 

I Can...

- [ ] read the 1st sentence.
- [ ] read the 2nd sentence.
- [ ] read the 3rd sentence.
- [ ] make my own sentence.
- [ ] color a picture.

Die Ziege hat einen Freund.

Geiten har en venn.

The goat has a friend.

Die Ziege hat vier Hufe.

Geiten har fire høver.

The goat has four hooves.

Name

I Can...

- [ ] read the 1st sentence.
- [ ] read the 2nd sentence.
- [ ] read the 3rd sentence.
- [ ] make my own sentence.
- [ ] color a picture.

Die Freundin meiner Mutter ist eine Magd.

Min venns venn er en hushjelp.

My mom's friend is a maid.

Die Magd hat einen großen braunen Besen.

Hushjelpen har en stor brun kost.

The maid has a big brown broom.

Name ____________________ 

I Can...

- ☐ read the 1st sentence.
- ☐ read the 2nd sentence.
- ☐ read the 3rd sentence.
- ☐ make my own sentence.
- ☐ color a picture.

Ich bin in den Zoo gegangen.

Jeg dro til dyrehagen.

I went to the zoo.

Die Tiere luden den Affen und den Papagei zum Übernachten ein.

Dyrene inviterte apen og papegøyen til å bli med på søvn.

The animals invited the monkey and the parrot to join their sleepover.

Name ___________________ 

I Can...

- ☐ read the 1st sentence.
- ☐ read the 2nd sentence.
- ☐ read the 3rd sentence.
- ☐ make my own sentence.
- ☐ color a picture.

Der Dinosaurier hat ein Kissen.

Dinosauren har en pute.

The dinosaur has a pillow.

Der Dinosaurier bekommt einen Teller für sein Essen.

Dinosauren skaffer seg en tallerken for maten.

The dinosaur is getting a plate for his food.

Name

I Can...

- [ ] read the 1st sentence.
- [ ] read the 2nd sentence.
- [ ] read the 3rd sentence.
- [ ] make my own sentence.
- [ ] color a picture.

Der Junge freut sich auf den Schulbesuch.

Gutten er spent på å gå på skolen.

The boy is excited to go to school.

Der Junge bereitet sich auf die Schule vor.

Gutten forbereder seg på skolen.

The boy is preparing for school.

Name

I Can...

- [ ] read the 1st sentence.
- [ ] read the 2nd sentence.
- [ ] read the 3rd sentence.
- [ ] make my own sentence.
- [ ] color a picture.

Die Kinder im Schulbus gehen zur Schule.

Barna på skolebussen skal på skolen.

The kids on the school bus are going to school.

Die Kinder gehen in einem Bus zur Schule.

Barna går på skole på buss.

The children go to school on a bus.

Name

I Can...

- [ ] read the 1st sentence.
- [ ] read the 2nd sentence.
- [ ] read the 3rd sentence.
- [ ] make my own sentence.
- [ ] color a picture.

Die Kobra ist sehr schön.

Kobraen er veldig deilig.

The cobra is very lovely.

Die Anakonda ist die längste Schlange der Welt.

Anacondaen er den lengste slangen i verden.

The anaconda is the longest snake in the world.

Name

I Can...

- [ ] read the 1st sentence.
- [ ] read the 2nd sentence.
- [ ] read the 3rd sentence.
- [ ] make my own sentence.
- [ ] color a picture.

Das ist ein fetter Hund!

Det er en feit hund!

That is a fat dog!

Der Hund hat ein goldenes Halsband.

Hunden har en gylden krage.

The dog has a golden collar.

Name

I Can...

- [ ] read the 1st sentence.
- [ ] read the 2nd sentence.
- [ ] read the 3rd sentence.
- [ ] make my own sentence.
- [ ] color a picture.

Der Elefant lebt im Zoo.

Elefanten bor i dyrehagen.

The elephant lives in the zoo.

Der Elefant hat einen langen Stamm.

Elefanten har en lang bagasjerom.

The elephant has a long trunk.

Name

I Can...

- [ ] read the 1st sentence.
- [ ] read the 2nd sentence.
- [ ] read the 3rd sentence.
- [ ] make my own sentence.
- [ ] color a picture.

Die Giraffe isst Gemüse.

Sjiraffen spiser grønnsaker.

The giraffe eats vegetables.

Die Giraffe hat viele Stellen.

Sjiraffen har mange flekker.

The giraffe has many spots.

Name ______________________

I Can...

- ☐ read the 1st sentence.
- ☐ read the 2nd sentence.
- ☐ read the 3rd sentence.
- ☐ make my own sentence.
- ☐ color a picture.

Der Chipmunk hat einen weichen Bauch.

Chipmunk har en myk mage.

The chipmunk has a soft tummy.

Der Streifenhörnchen brachte eine riesige Eichel nach Hause.

Chipmunk brakte hjem en gigantisk eikenøtt.

The chipmunk brought home a giant acorn.

Name

I Can...

- [ ] read the 1st sentence.
- [ ] read the 2nd sentence.
- [ ] read the 3rd sentence.
- [ ] make my own sentence.
- [ ] color a picture.

Ich habe insgesamt zehn Zehen.

Jeg har ti tær totalt.

I have ten toes in total.

Eins und Null zusammen sind zehn.

One og Zero sammen er ti.

One and Zero together are ten.

Name ____________________ 

I Can...

- ☐ read the 1st sentence.
- ☐ read the 2nd sentence.
- ☐ read the 3rd sentence.
- ☐ make my own sentence.
- ☐ color a picture.

Der Alligator springt.

Alligatoren hopper.

The alligator is jumping.

Das springende Krokodil ist glücklich.

Den hoppende krokodillen er fornøyd.

The jumping crocodile is happy.

Name

I Can...

- ☐ read the 1st sentence.
- ☐ read the 2nd sentence.
- ☐ read the 3rd sentence.
- ☐ make my own sentence.
- ☐ color a picture.

Ich habe eine Ameise gefunden.

Jeg fant en maur.

I found an ant.

Eine Ameise ist klein, aber sehr stark.

En maur er liten i størrelse, men veldig sterk.

An ant is tiny in size, but very strong.

Name ____________________ 

85

I Can...

- [ ] read the 1st sentence.
- [ ] read the 2nd sentence.
- [ ] read the 3rd sentence.
- [ ] make my own sentence.
- [ ] color a picture.

Die Fledermaus schläft verkehrt herum.

Flaggermusen sover opp ned.

The bat sleeps upside down.

Die Fledermaus umarmt den Brief.

Flaggermusen klemmer brevet.

The bat is hugging the letter.

Name ____________________

I Can...

- [ ] read the 1st sentence.
- [ ] read the 2nd sentence.
- [ ] read the 3rd sentence.
- [ ] make my own sentence.
- [ ] color a picture.

Die Katze ist sehr müde.

Katten er veldig sliten.

The cat is very tired.

Die Katze ist sehr müde.

Katten er veldig søvnig.

The cat is very sleepy.

Name

I Can...

- [ ] read the 1st sentence.
- [ ] read the 2nd sentence.
- [ ] read the 3rd sentence.
- [ ] make my own sentence.
- [ ] color a picture.

Der Hund spielt gern.

Hunden liker å leke.

The dog likes to play.

Der Hund leckt gerne den Knochen.

Hunden liker å slikke beinet.

The dog likes to lick the bone.

Name

I Can...

- [ ] read the 1st sentence.
- [ ] read the 2nd sentence.
- [ ] read the 3rd sentence.
- [ ] make my own sentence.
- [ ] color a picture.

Der Elefant hat Wimpern.

Elefanten har øyevipper.

The elephant has eyelashes.

Der Elefant hat große Ohren.

Elefanten har store ører.

The elephant has big ears.

Name _______________________ 

I Can...

- [ ] read the 1st sentence.
- [ ] read the 2nd sentence.
- [ ] read the 3rd sentence.
- [ ] make my own sentence.
- [ ] color a picture.

Der Frosch hüpft.

Frosken hopper.

The frog is hopping.

Der Frosch nutzt seine Zunge, um Beute zu fangen.

Frosken bruker tungen for å fange byttedyr.

The frog uses its tongue to catch prey.

Name

I Can...

- [ ] read the 1st sentence.
- [ ] read the 2nd sentence.
- [ ] read the 3rd sentence.
- [ ] make my own sentence.
- [ ] color a picture.

Die Ziege läuft müde herum.

Geita går søvnig rundt.

The goat is sleepily walking around.

Die Ziege weidet auf der Wiese.

Geita beiter på engen.

The goat is grazing in the meadow.

Name ______________________

I Can...

- [ ] read the 1st sentence.
- [ ] read the 2nd sentence.
- [ ] read the 3rd sentence.
- [ ] make my own sentence.
- [ ] color a picture.

Das Nilpferd hat einen großen Kopf.

Flodhesten har et stort hode.

The hippo has a big head.

Das Nilpferd ist erstaunt, wie groß seine Zähne sind.

Flodhesten er overrasket over hvor store tennene hans er.

The hippo is amazed at how big his teeth are.

Name

I Can...

- [ ] read the 1st sentence.
- [ ] read the 2nd sentence.
- [ ] read the 3rd sentence.
- [ ] make my own sentence.
- [ ] color a picture.

Der Leguan hat einen langen Schwanz.

Leguanen har en lang hale.

The iguana has a long tail.

Der Leguan kräuselt sich um das Alphabet.

Leguanen krøller seg rundt alfabetet.

The iguana is curling around the alphabet.

Name

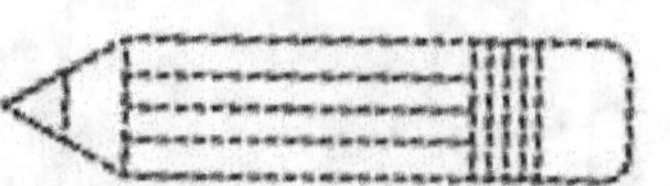

I Can...

- [ ] read the 1st sentence.
- [ ] read the 2nd sentence.
- [ ] read the 3rd sentence.
- [ ] make my own sentence.
- [ ] color a picture.

Mama kaufte eine neue Flasche Marmelade.

Mamma kjøpte en ny flaske syltetøy.

Mom bought a new bottle of jam.

Sie können Marmelade auf Toast geben, um ihm mehr Geschmack zu verleihen.

Du kan legge syltetøy på toast for å gi den mer smak.

You can put jam on toast to give it more taste.

Name

I Can...

- [ ] read the 1st sentence.
- [ ] read the 2nd sentence.
- [ ] read the 3rd sentence.
- [ ] make my own sentence.
- [ ] color a picture.

Der Drachen hat einen schönen Schwanz.

Kiten har en vakker hale.

The kite has a beautiful tail.

Der Drachen ist am Boden.

Kiten er på bakken.

The kite is on the ground.

Name ______________________________

I Can...

- ☐ read the 1st sentence.
- ☐ read the 2nd sentence.
- ☐ read the 3rd sentence.
- ☐ make my own sentence.
- ☐ color a picture.

Der Löwe ist schüchtern.

Løven er redd.

The lion is timid.

Der Löwe jagt seinen Schwanz.

Løven jager halen.

The lion is chasing its tail.

Name ____________________ 

I Can...

- [ ] read the 1st sentence.
- [ ] read the 2nd sentence.
- [ ] read the 3rd sentence.
- [ ] make my own sentence.
- [ ] color a picture.

Ich mag Mäuse.

Jeg liker mus.

I like mice.

Die Maus hat sehr lange Schnurrhaare.

Musen har veldig lange værhår.

The mouse has very long whiskers.

Name

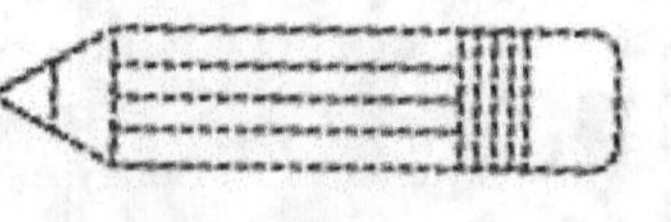

I Can...

- [ ] read the 1st sentence.
- [ ] read the 2nd sentence.
- [ ] read the 3rd sentence.
- [ ] make my own sentence.
- [ ] color a picture.

Die Nase atmet.

Nesen puster.

The nose is breathing.

Die Nase dient zum Riechen von Dingen.

Nesen brukes til å lukte ting.

The nose is used for smelling things.

Name

I Can...

- [ ] read the 1st sentence.
- [ ] read the 2nd sentence.
- [ ] read the 3rd sentence.
- [ ] make my own sentence.
- [ ] color a picture.

Der Oktopus lebt unter Wasser.

Blekkspruten lever under vann.

The octopus lives underwater.

Die Krake hat sehr lange Tentakeln.

Blekkspruten har veldig lange tentakler.

The octopus has very long tentacles.

Name ___________________ 

I Can...

- [ ] read the 1st sentence.
- [ ] read the 2nd sentence.
- [ ] read the 3rd sentence.
- [ ] make my own sentence.
- [ ] color a picture.

Der Pinguin frisst Fisch.

Pingvinen spiser fisk.

The penguin eats fish.

Der Pinguin lebt in kalten Regionen.

Pingvinen bor i kalde strøk.

The penguin lives in cold regions.

Name

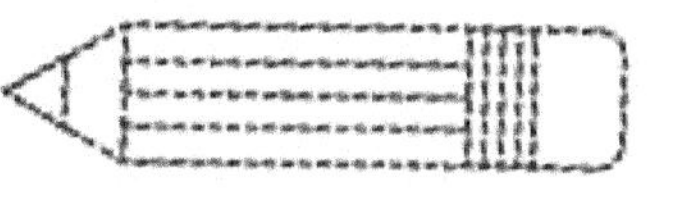

I Can...

- [ ] read the 1st sentence.
- [ ] read the 2nd sentence.
- [ ] read the 3rd sentence.
- [ ] make my own sentence.
- [ ] color a picture.

Die Königin hat einen Zauberstab.

Dronningen har en tryllestav.

The queen has a wand.

Die Königin hat einen rosa Zauberstab.

Dronningen har en rosa stav.

The queen has a pink wand.

Name ________________________ 

I Can...

- [ ] read the 1st sentence.
- [ ] read the 2nd sentence.
- [ ] read the 3rd sentence.
- [ ] make my own sentence.
- [ ] color a picture.

Der Hase hat lange Ohren.

Kaninen har lange ører.

The rabbit has long ears.

Der Hase ist verwirrt.

Kaninen er forvirret.

The rabbit is confused.

Name

I Can...

- [ ] read the 1st sentence.
- [ ] read the 2nd sentence.
- [ ] read the 3rd sentence.
- [ ] make my own sentence.
- [ ] color a picture.

Die Schlange hat I upfen.

Slangen har prikker.

I he snake has polka dots.

Die Schlange ist sehr schleimig.

Slangen er veldig slim.

I he snake is very slimy.

Name

I Can...

- [ ] read the 1st sentence.
- [ ] read the 2nd sentence.
- [ ] read the 3rd sentence.
- [ ] make my own sentence.
- [ ] color a picture.

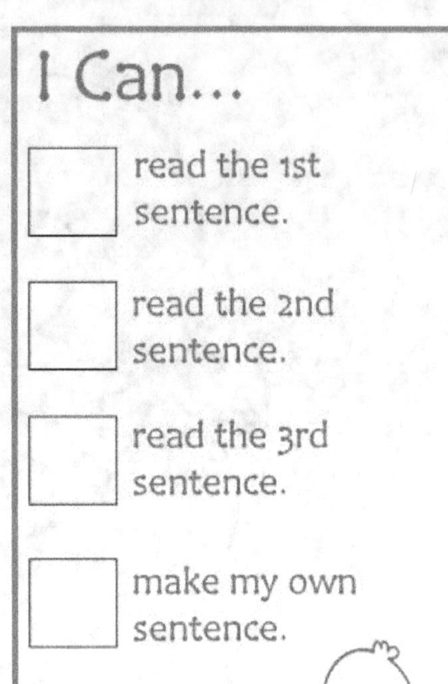

Die Schildkröte hat eine spitze Schale.

Skilpadden har et spisse skall.

The tortoise has a pointy shell.

Die Schildkröte lebt an Land, im Gegensatz zu Schildkröten.

Skilpadden lever på land, i motsetning til skilpadder.

The tortoise lives on land, unlike turtles.

Name

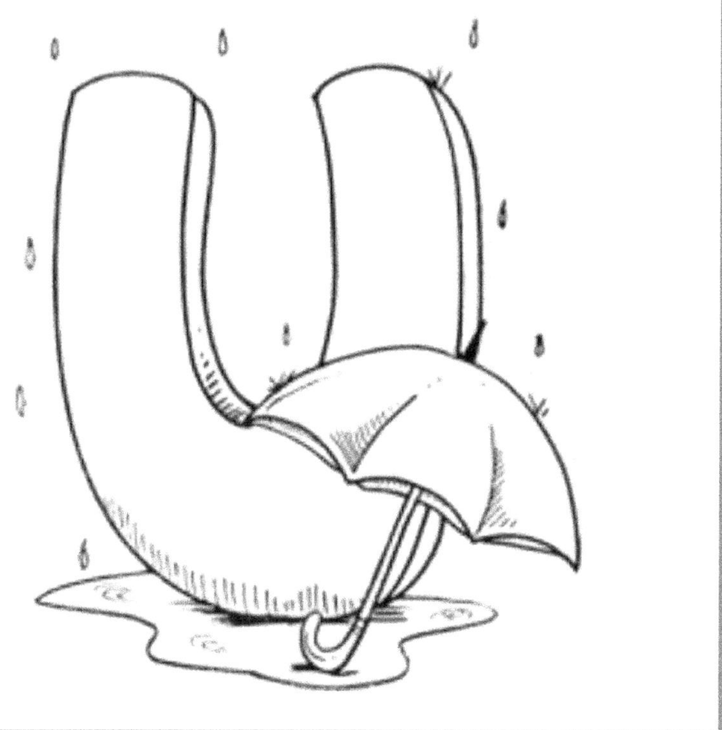

I Can...

- [ ] read the 1st sentence.
- [ ] read the 2nd sentence.
- [ ] read the 3rd sentence.
- [ ] make my own sentence.
- [ ] color a picture.

Es regnet.

Det regner.

It's raining.

Der Regenschirm schützt dich.

Paraplyen skjuler deg.

The umbrella shelters you.

Name

I Can...

- [ ] read the 1st sentence.
- [ ] read the 2nd sentence.
- [ ] read the 3rd sentence.
- [ ] make my own sentence.
- [ ] color a picture.

Die Geige ist ein Musikinstrument.

Fiolinen er et musikkinstrument.

The violin is a musical instrument.

Die Geige ist eines der fantastischsten Instrumente.

Fiolin er et av de mest fantastiske instrumentene.

The violin is one of the most fantastic instruments.

Name _______________________

I Can...

- [ ] read the 1st sentence.
- [ ] read the 2nd sentence.
- [ ] read the 3rd sentence.
- [ ] make my own sentence.
- [ ] color a picture.

Das Walross hat einen Freund.

Hvalrossen har en venn.

The walrus has a friend.

Das Walross hat einen Schwanz.

Hvalrossen har en hale.

The walrus has a tail.

Name

I Can...

- [ ] read the 1st sentence.
- [ ] read the 2nd sentence.
- [ ] read the 3rd sentence.
- [ ] make my own sentence.
- [ ] color a picture.

Das Xylophon ist ein buntes Instrument.

Xylofonen er et fargerikt instrument.

The xylophone is a colorful instrument.

Das Xylophon ist ein sehr cooles Instrument.

Xylofonen er et veldig kult instrument.

The xylophone is a very cool instrument.

Name

I Can...

- [ ] read the 1st sentence.
- [ ] read the 2nd sentence.
- [ ] read the 3rd sentence.
- [ ] make my own sentence.
- [ ] color a picture.

Der Junge hat einen kleinen Hut.

Gutten har en liten hatt.

The boy has a little hat.

Das Kind hat ein sehr buntes Jojo.

Barnet har en veldig fargerik yoyo.

The kid has a very colorful yoyo.

Name

I Can...

- [ ] read the 1st sentence.
- [ ] read the 2nd sentence.
- [ ] read the 3rd sentence.
- [ ] make my own sentence.
- [ ] color a picture.

Das Zebra hat einen Schwanz.

Sebraen har en hale.

The zebra has a tail.

Das Zebra lächelt weit

Sebraen smiler bredt

The zebra is smiling widely

Name

I Can...

- [ ] read the 1st sentence.
- [ ] read the 2nd sentence.
- [ ] read the 3rd sentence.
- [ ] make my own sentence.
- [ ] color a picture.

Ich habe eine Kerze auf meinem Kuchen.

Jeg har et lys på kaken.

I have a candle on my cake.

Diese Geburtstagstorte ist für ein kleines Kind.

Denne bursdagskaken er for et lite barn.

This birthday cake is for a little kids.

Name _______________________

I Can...

- ☐ read the 1st sentence.
- ☐ read the 2nd sentence.
- ☐ read the 3rd sentence.
- ☐ make my own sentence.
- ☐ color a picture.

Der Astronaut ist auf Mission.

Astronauten skal på oppdrag.

The astronaut is going on a mission.

Der Astronaut sah etwas in der Ferne.

Astronauten så noe i det fjerne.

The astronaut saw something in the distance.

Name 

I Can...

- [ ] read the 1st sentence.
- [ ] read the 2nd sentence.
- [ ] read the 3rd sentence.
- [ ] make my own sentence.
- [ ] color a picture.

Der Samurai geht morgens joggen.

Samurai skal på morgenjoggetur.

The samurai is going for a morning jog.

Der Samurai jagt seinen Feind weg.

Samuraien jager bort fienden.

The samurai is chasing away his enemy.

Name _______________________ 

I Can...

- [ ] read the 1st sentence.
- [ ] read the 2nd sentence.
- [ ] read the 3rd sentence.
- [ ] make my own sentence.
- [ ] color a picture.

Mein Freund hat einen riesigen Kuchen.

Venninnen min har en gigantisk kake.

My friend is having a gigantic cake.

Diese Geburtstagstorte hat drei Schichten.

Denne bursdagskaken har tre lag.

This birthday cake has three layers.

I Can...

- ☐ read the 1st sentence.
- ☐ read the 2nd sentence.
- ☐ read the 3rd sentence.
- ☐ make my own sentence.
- ☐ color a picture.

Der Frosch jagt die Fliege.

Frosken jager flua.

The frog is chasing the fly.

Der Frosch fängt eine Fliege.

Frosken fanger en flue.

The frog is catching a fly.

Name

I Can...

- [ ] read the 1st sentence.
- [ ] read the 2nd sentence.
- [ ] read the 3rd sentence.
- [ ] make my own sentence.
- [ ] color a picture.

Der Marienkäfer hat sechs Beine.

Marihøna har seks bein.

The ladybug has six legs.

Der Marienkäfer lächelt.

Marihøna smiler.

The ladybug is smiling.

Name

I Can...

- [ ] read the 1st sentence.
- [ ] read the 2nd sentence.
- [ ] read the 3rd sentence.
- [ ] make my own sentence.
- [ ] color a picture.

Der Drache ist krank.

Dragen er syk.

The dragon is sick.

Der Drache ist sehr durstig.

Dragen er veldig tørst.

The dragon is very thirsty.

Name _________________________

I Can...

- [ ] read the 1st sentence.
- [ ] read the 2nd sentence.
- [ ] read the 3rd sentence.
- [ ] make my own sentence.
- [ ] color a picture.

Das ist eine kleine Kuh.

Det er en baby-ku.

That is a baby cow.

Das Kalb irrt herum.

Kalven vandrer rundt.

The calf is wandering around.